How to Build a Deck

Step-by-Step Instructions

How to Build a Deck

Step-by-Step Instructions

CJ Dodaro

This is a self-published book.

First Edition

Illustrated

Published: November 2020

ISBN: 9798566080369

Other titles by CJ Dodaro:

Being Successful in Your Own Business - A Step-by-Step Guide to Success

(This is a (3) Book Series)

Book 1 of 3 in the Series: Your Business Setup

Book 2 of 3 in the Series: Work on Your Website

Book 3 of 3 in the Series: Get Social, Videos, and Money Management

<u>**Book 4:**</u> <u>**Write it - Publish it - FREE!**</u>

<u>**Book 5:**</u> <u>**Make Money - Work at Home with an Unclaimed Money Recovery Business**</u>

<u>**Book 6:**</u> <u>**Make Money - Work at Home with a Tax Sale Overages Business**</u>

<u>**Book 7:**</u> <u>**Make Money - Work at Home with a Tax Lien Certificates & Tax Deeds Business**</u>

<u>Dedication</u>

This book is dedicated to all those that helped me complete this project. In no particular order: my friend, **Steve**, who helped tremendously by hand digging the holes for the concrete pillars, as well as, installing the needed wallboard, taping, mudding, and painting the inside room, my good friend and neighbor, **Jim**, who was a great help with the concrete work, framework, and decking, to my Grandson, **Devon**, who was instrumental by assisting throughout the project, Devon's girlfriend, **Fia**, who assisted with various parts of the project, my daughter, **Jenifer**, who chose and picked up the paint and molding for the inside and taped all of the trim work, and last, but certainly, not least, my wife, **Karen**, who was there daily, keeping us hydrated, bringing us lunch, and helping me clean up at the end of each day.

x

Table of Contents

Table of Contents (cont')

xiii

How to Build a Deck

Step-by-Step Instructions

Introduction

Building a deck can be an exciting and useful project, one that you can enjoy for many years to come. However, if you cut corners when working on your project, you run the risk of not passing inspections and/or compromising the safety of yourself and anyone else that would use your deck. I highly recommend that you follow the guidelines contained in this book, as well as, the ordinances in your city or town so that your project will produce the intended results of many years of safe happiness.

This book is a step-by-step guide which will walk you through the building of your deck in a simple, easy to follow manner. The project contained herein is for a 16' x 16' deck. If you intend to build yours a different size, all you will need to do is make some adjustments to the products needed list, as well as, to certain points in the construction to fit your situation. There are suggestions contained in each appropriate chapter to compensate for any differences.

I wish you the best of luck in your project, and many happy years of use upon completion.

Thank you for purchasing this book, and I wish you all the best in your new venture.

Sincerely,

CJ Dodaro

Chapter 1: <u>Making Decisions</u>

Karen's Completed Deck

<u>Safety</u>

Before I get into this project, I would like to talk to you a little about safety. There are several points that I would like to make:

1. <u>Treated Lumber</u> - Treated lumber is treated with somewhat hazardous materials in order to preserve it. While it is relatively safe to use, you should take the following precautions:

   a. Always wear gloves when handling it. Also, do not walk barefoot on it.

   b. Always wear a dust mask when cutting or sanding it.

   c. Always wear safety glasses when cutting it, along with a hat.

2. <u>Power Tools</u> - While the use of power tools such as saws and drills are very useful for the speediness of completing your project, certain extra precautions should be used:

   a. Always wear tight fitting gloves when operating a power tool and grip the tool firmly with both hands.

   b. Keep moving parts such as blades and bits away from gloves, fingers, and other body parts.

c. Always clamp wood to your saw horses before attempting to cut it to prevent movement and instability.

d. Always use sharp blades and bits and do your cuts and drilling slow and steady. Do not force the tool to do more work than it is capable of by trying to rush it.

e. Always use safety glasses and dust masks when cutting and drilling.

3. <u>Ladders and Stools</u> - Using ladders and stools are sometimes necessary in order to complete certain aspects of a project. However, observe the following:

a. Always make sure that your ladder or stool is on firm ground and level. Support the legs with wide blocks of wood if necessary.

b. Always maintain 3 - point contact while ascending or descending a ladder or stool; 2 feet and 1 hand or 1 foot and 2 hands.

c. Never overreach while on a ladder or stool. Take the time to climb down and move the ladder closer to your work area.

Disclaimer

CJ Dodaro and/or Improving America LLC assumes no responsibility for errors or accidents in a project by anyone using these instructions to work on their project. All individuals are responsible for their own actions, and safety should always be a priority.

Decisions to be Made

Be advised that our deck is being installed on a raised ranch house with hardboard siding. If your house is different, say, aluminum siding or brick, then, you will need to search the internet to see what you will need to do in order to attach your ledger board to the house.

Before you build your deck, you have certain decisions to make. These will include: location, size, material type, etc. First, location should be addressed.

Location

Assuming your deck will be installed in your back yard, you should pick a location allowing you easy access to it. If you do not have a back door allowing this access, not to worry. We will be installing one later as part of this project.

The deck we installed was off of the living room in a raised ranch. The room already had a large picture window in it, overlooking the back yard, so there was already a header in place. If this is your situation, perfect. If not, you will need to decide where in the room you would like to cut a hole for your new access door. This door will be 6' wide, and can either be a sliding patio door or French doors, whichever you prefer. You can either install your deck off of your living room or kitchen (whichever is located at the back of your home) or a bedroom. If choosing a bedroom, be aware that this would require any guests that you have over to enter and leave your deck through this room, so this is usually not the ideal choice.

You should also keep in mind any plants that may already be in the area where you will install your deck. These will need to removed and either transplanted elsewhere on your property, given to a neighbor, or merely thrown away if necessary. We transplanted a dozen or so yuccas and twice as many hostas. We also gave some plants away to the neighbor. We put in a small retaining wall building a back bed to hold the plants, along with all of the dirt that we removed for the deck.

Fia & Devon Digging Trench for Retaining Wall

Completed Back Bed - Retaining Wall & Plants

You should also be aware of any air conditioning unit in the area. You will not be able to install your deck over one, so if it is present in your proposed area, you will need to have it relocated elsewhere. You should hire a heating and air conditioning specialist to perform this task.

Size

Once the location for your door has been decided, you will need to decide on the size of your deck. Remember, boards generally come in lengths of 2' increments, so to eliminate a lot of waste, you should choose the size to be anywhere from 8' to 20' wide and long as you desire. Our deck was 16' x 16'. Your deck can either be square like we chose or a rectangle if that suits you better.

While a 12' x 12' deck may seem originally sufficient, you should take into consideration what you will place on your deck and how many people may be using it at one time. You will probably be putting some type of table along with seating, perhaps a barbeque grill, perhaps an umbrella, and possibly a storage box for chair cushions. Be sure that you will have enough comfortable walking room around all of your items. Usually a 12' x 12' deck is suitable for 2 people to comfortably use, but a minimum of a 16' x 16' deck is recommended for a family of 4 - 8 people.

Material to be Used

Next, you will need to decide on the type of material for your deck: treated lumber, composite, or a combination of both. If combining, you would generally use treated lumber for your framework and composite for your deck boards. Composite material, while quite nice, is very costly; usually triple the price of treated lumber, so you may choose to use treated lumber as we did. However, keep in mind, that due to the Covid 19 pandemic, treated lumber is much harder to come by these days, and the prices have gone up according to the supply and demand in any given area. We had to go to (6) different big box stores to get everything that we needed. We spent all day, renting a truck and picking it up. That was a better alternative than to spend a ton of money on multiple deliveries, and needing to return any unwanted warp or excessively knotty wood. You will need to check availability in your area to see if this will be a factor for you.

Deck Plans for Free

Once these decisions have been made, you can go to a big box store like Lowes, Home Depot, or Menards and for free, they will draw you a plan of your deck and give you a materials list and approximate cost. Do not use this as your final plan however; they usually are not exactly accurate. These types of plans are meant to only give you an idea of how things might be laid out.

You will probably need to get several permits from your city or town prior to installing your deck, which should also give you some ideas about what specifically may be required of you in your area to be compliant. You will probably need individual permits for: access door, deck, concrete slab at base of stairs, and any electric work that you intend to do, such as, installing a light and/or receptacle. These permits will usually cost you between $300 - $500 total.

You will also need to provide a plot of survey for your property. This is usually found with your home financing papers or you can contact your County and obtain a free copy.

You do not have to be a master carpenter to build a deck, but familiarity with certain tools, like a skill saw, chain saw, and a drill, will be very helpful.

Sketches

Once these decisions have been made, it is time to sketch drawings of the different aspects of your deck. These will include: posts placement, ledgers and joists, stairs, and railings. You should include dimensions where appropriate, some of which you will not know until later on in this book, but you should initially fill in what you can, such as overall dimensions of your proposed deck and width and location of your stairs. For our purposes here, we are building a 16' x 16' deck for a raised ranch, which will be approximately 5' above ground level. All of our ledgers, joists, and posts will be based on this. If you are building a deck off of a ranch home, than posts placement and stairs can be eliminated.

You will need at least one or two helpers to complete this project. Choose individuals that you can count on to be there every day that you will be working on your project.

Once your sketches have been made, and you received information from your city or town on deck specifications, it will be time to move on to the next Step: **Chapter 2: List of Needed Materials and Supplies**.

Chapter 2: <u>List of Needed Materials and Supplies</u>

Covered Materials & Karen

Again, our list of materials is based on the deck we are building, which is 16' x 16', 5' above ground. Any variation for your deck will require you to adjust your materials and supplies list, as well as, some of the steps for building.

16' and larger decks require a couple of things that smaller decks will not need. These are: 6" posts with 12" diameter holes compared to 4" posts with 10" diameter holes for smaller desks. Also, 16' and larger decks require a double cross beam in the center, which are not required for 12' and smaller decks.

For our deck, ledger boards will be 2" x 10"s and joists will be 2" x 8"s. This will make the deck nice and solid. We will also be using cross boards in between our joists at 4' and 12' from the house. This will also create a more solid deck. Cross bracing will not be needed between our posts since we are using 6" x 6"s. If you use 4" x 4"s for a smaller deck, this is recommended. These braces will be placed at a 45 degree angle from top of one post to the bottom of the adjoining post.

Also, for all decks, I recommend using 5/4 boards for decking and railings as opposed to 3/4" boards. This will make it more solid and will tend not to warp as much.

Create a spreadsheet for your materials list. Here is the materials list for our deck (you should create a similar one for your deck):

Materials List for Karen's Deck

Access Door

1 - 6' wide door

4 - 2" x 4" x 8'

1 - 4' x 8' sheet of 1/2" wallboard

1 - package of shims

1 - roll of insulation

1 - can of expandable foam

20' - interior trim

20' - exterior trim

1 - roll of wallboard tape

1 - bucket of patching compound

1 - roll of painter's tape

1 - gallon of wallboard primer

2 - gallons of paint (amount may vary by room size)

3 - tubes of silicone caulk

Foundation & Flatwork

3 - 6" x 6" x 10' posts (cut in half)

8 - 4" x 4" x 8' posts

1 - 10" post tube (for stairs) at least 4' long

6 - 12" post tubes at least 4' long

64 bags - 5000 psi concrete mix

111 - 4" x 8" Charcoal Bricks (for perimeter of deck)

4 bags - levelling sand

3 - Rolls of weed block (enough to cover your under-the-deck area)

100 - Staples to pin down the weed block (2 staples every 4' - 1 at each end)

2 tons pea gravel (for under deck)

12 bags - limestone screening (for slab base)

2 - 1" x 8" x 10' treated (for slab framework)

Framework

1 - 12" x 25' flashing membrane (for ledger board)

1 - 4" x 75' flashing membrane tape (for door and patching)

2 - 10' aluminum white flashing (for ledger/door drip edge)

6 - 2" x 10" x 16' treated (for ledgers and beam)

11 - 2" x 8" x 16' treated (for joists)

2 - 2" x 8" x 14' treated (for cross braces)

1 - 4' x 4' sheet of fiber board (if needed)

1 - small roll of tar paper

Decking and Railings

38 - 5/4" x 6" x 16' treated (for decking and railings)

44 - 36" spindles

Stairs and Stair Railing

4 - 8 step stringers treated

4 - 1" x 8" x 10' treated (for risers)

10 - 5/4" x 6" x 10' treated (8 - cut in half for steps, 2 for stair railing)

6 - 4" x 4" x 8' treated (posts for railing and stairs - top)

4 - 4" x 4" x 6' treated (posts for stair railing - bottom and center)

99 - 36" spindles

2 - 10' - 2" diameter hand rails

<u>Hardware</u>

1 - 1 lb. box of 2" finishing nails

1 - 1 lb. box of 1 5/8" wallboard screws

1 - 1 lb. box of 1 1/2" roofing nails

6 - 6" x 6" post anchors with cover tops

1 - 4" x 4" post anchor with cover top

7 - J - 1/2" post anchor bolts

22 - 8" joist hangers

4 - 8" corner hangers

11 - rafter ties

1 - 50 count box of 3 5/8" ledger lok screws

4 - stair stringer hangers

20 - 8" - 1/2" galvanized or stainless steel bolts

24 - 6" - 1/2" galvanized stainless steel bolts

88 - 1/2" flat washers

44 - 1/2" lock washers

44 - 1/2" lock nuts

1 - 550 count box of 1 1/2" galvanized nails

7 - 3/8" - 1 1/2" long lag screws

2 - 900 count boxes of 2 1/2" deck screws (gold)

1 - 1 lb. box of 1 1/2" deck screws (gold)

8 - hand rail brackets with screws

Make whatever adjustments may be necessary based on your deck size.

I suggest that you create a spreadsheet for your materials list. Create columns for: Quantity, Description, Cost Each, and Total Cost. Then, for the Cost, compare each item with several big box stores like Lowes, Menards, and Home Depot, along with a couple local lumber yards in order to see who will give you the best deals. You can either have the goods delivered or rent a cargo van and pick everything up yourself; your choice. I preferred to hand pick all of my material so that I could avoid as many knots, imperfections, and warped boards as possible. If you choose to take your chances and have the goods delivered, be sure to verify the return policy of the places that you order from and order 10% - 20% more than what you need so that you can return the boards that are unacceptable.

Do not order your materials yet, just collect prices and check availability. You still have a couple of other steps to complete first.

The next **Step** will be to make a **Tools Needed List**.

Chapter 3: <u>List of Tools Needed</u>

Now it is time to make a list of all of the tools that you will need. You should have a table or two to place them on, preferably in your garage or shed, where you can keep them in case it rains. You can have a separate table outside for when you are working.

<u>Rentals</u>

You should minimally rent a sod cutter (unless your deck is very small). In the case of a small deck, you can scrape up the sod by hand if you so choose.

You can rent a post hole digger and/or a concrete mixer if you so desire. We chose to dig our holes by hand and mix our concrete 2 bags at a time in a wheel barrow.

Sod Cutter

Post Hole Digger with 42" bit

Concrete Mixer

<u>Tools</u>

Stud Finder

1/2" Drill Bit

Wallboard Hand Saw

4" putty knife

Nail set

Stanley Knife with sharp blade

Wet/dry sponge

Empty bucket

Flat Spade

Hand Post Hole Digger

Curved Spade

Rototiller

Wheel Barrow

Long Handled Flat Shovel

2 - Short Handled Flat Shovels

Concrete Float

Screed Board (level 2" x 4" x 6')

Claw Hammer

Screw/Nail Apron

Rubber Mallet

Hack Saw

Chain Saw with sharp blade

Gas Mixture (if gas powered chain saw)

Chain Saw Oil

4" Flat Chisel (heavy duty)

Battery Operated Drill w/at least 2 batteries and charger

Electric Drill

Set of 3/8" - 1" Hole Bits (at least 8" long)

Drill Bit slightly smaller than your 2 1/2" screw shank (all holes should be pre-drilled before screwing)

Skill Saw w/crosscut/rip combination blade

Hand Tamper

4 - Adjustable Clamps (opening at least 6")

10" Chop/Miter Saw with crosscut blade

Hand Saw

Timber Lok or Ledger Lok Driver Bit

Deck Screw Bit

3/8" Ratchet with 3/4" deep well socket (or cordless ratchet)

3/4" Boxed End Wrench

48" T-Square

12" T-Square

Post Level

4' Level

Line Level

Chalked String Line

100' of Stretchable Line

18 - 2' Stakes

8 - 12" Stakes

2 - Saw Horses

Plumb Line with at least 6' of string

Small Curved Pry Bar

25' Tape Measure

100' Cloth Tape Measure

Electric Sawsall w/short and long blades

7 screwdrivers (any type)

1 - Phillips screwdriver

Can of Marking Paint (for your post holes)

Garden Hose with Spray Nozzle (must reach the work site)

Several 50' extension cords

Multi-Outlet Surge Bar

Caulk Gun

8" long, thin, poking rod (to break the seal in the caulk tube)

3 - empty 5 gallon buckets for wood chips and sawdust

2 - Pencils

Once you have all of your tools, arrange them on your tables. Now it is time to mark out the area for your new deck.

Chapter 4: <u>Preparing the Area for Your Deck</u>

<u>Mark Your House For Your Ledger Board</u>

Now it is time to mark out the area for your deck. The first thing to do is to measure 1" below the threshold of your access door (if you are using 5/4" boards for your decking, which are actually 1" thick) and make a mark near both ends of your threshold.

Now, take your 4' level, beginning at your mark on one side and make a level mark every 4' until you reach the end of your home (if you are putting your deck near the edge of your home). You should start your deck about 1' in from the edge of your home if your deck is going up near the edge. It will look more aesthetically pleasing than going to the edge of the house with your deck. Make a pencil mark at the top about 1' in from the edge of your home, and even with your top mark for your ledger. If you are not putting your deck near the end of your home, make marks out to approximately where your deck will end on one side.

Then, take your 25' tape measure and measure from the end mark (marking the one end of your ledger), the width of your deck (in our case - 16') and make another pencil mark. Make sure that your tape measure is as level as possible. Double check level with your 4' level in the same way you did the other side. Remark if needed, and erase the old.

Now, measure down 9 3/4" from each top mark and make a pencil mark there. Make sure that your marks are level. Connect the marks with a pencil mark on both ends. Then, take your chalk line, and snap a line between your 2 upper marks and another line between your 2 lower marks.

Take your plumb line and hold it against each vertical line marking your ledger board ends, stop it from swaying, and make a pencil mark (which should be level) on your foundation on each side. Double check the mark with your 4' level on both sides.

<u>Mark Out For Your Deck</u>

The next thing that you need to do is to mark the perimeter for your deck with stakes. It is best to place the 1st two stakes, closest to the house with the outside edge of each of the stakes even with your marks on your foundation. Then, measure from the outside of 1 stake to the outside of the other. The distance should be equal to your ledger board (equal to your deck width).

Then, measure out the distance of the length of your deck from your house siding near each stake and pound in a new stake at these corners. You should have your helper stand about 20' from each of your proposed stake placements and tell you left or right until it looks level with the house. String out the perimeter with your stretchable string, placing the string about 4" - 6" above the ground and on the outside edge of your stakes. Be sure to wrap the string around each stake several times before going on to the next, pulling the string nice and tight and tying it off at the last stake. Now, take your large T-Square and check for squareness of your sides to the house on both ends of the width of your proposed deck area. Reposition your outside stakes as needed.

Now, take your 100' Cloth Tape Measure and have your helper hold one end at each corner of the stakes closest to the house at the outside corner of each stake and measure to the opposite outside corner of the opposing stake. The measurements should be equal if you are square. If not, double check your squareness with your T-Square on both sides from the house and adjust your outside stakes as needed. Remeasure your distances from corner to corner until you are equal. You can have your helper stand about 20' back from each outside stake to see if each side looks perpendicular to the house. Adjust your outside stakes and remeasure until you are satisfied.

Mark Out for Your Stairs

Now, you need to calculate your stair stringer distance based on your height and number of stairs that will be needed. Do this as follows:

1. **Start by finding the overall height that the staircase will be.** You can measure from the top of your proposed ledger board on the house to the ground.

2. **Decide the height or "rise" you'll want for each step.** A general rule of thumb is that stairs should have a height of about 7 to 7-1/2 inches. Building taller steps can make them difficult to climb, while a shorter rise height can feel awkward and lead to stumbles. Check the requirements with your town or city.

3. **Divide the total height of the staircase by the height or "rise" you want for each step.** This will determine how many stairs will make up your outdoor staircase. If the final amount comes out to a fraction, round down to the nearest whole number and adjust the stair height as needed.

4. **Run that formula again, however, divide the total height of the staircase now by the total number of steps.** Do not round the measurement at all. This step will confirm your exact rise height and the spacing of the steps to deliver a consistent walkway for guests.

5. **Determine how deep you want your steps to be and multiply that distance by the number of steps you'll have.** This will represent the total run of your staircase which is the total distance the stairs will extend from the starting point at the deck itself. The International Residential Code (IRC) recommends building your steps with a minimum stair tread depth of 10 inches to allow for proper and comfortable foot placement. If you are using 5/4" x 6" boards as we did, your boards will actually be about 5 1/2" wide, so 2 boards would equal 11" for your treads. These will probably hang over about 1" past your risers which is aesthetically pleasing.

6. **Lastly, with all of the dimensions in hand, sketch out your stair plans to get a clear vision for your stringer boards.** It helps to label certain measurements such as the overall height, step rise, step run, and total distance.

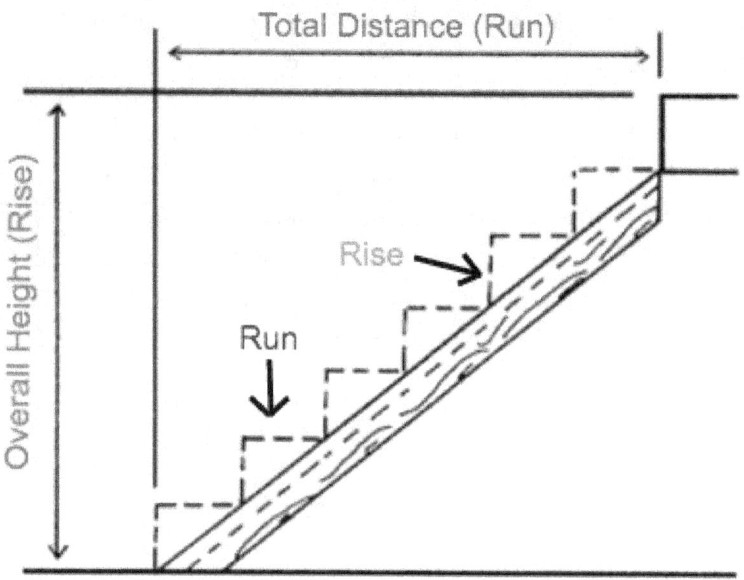

Once you have your deck square and your measurement for the length of your stairs, put in stakes where your stairs will be (at all 4 corners and using your T-Square, square up to your string line marking your deck. String out a line between your stair stakes and pull lines taught, placing your string line on the outside edge of your stakes. Tie off the final end. Adjust your stakes as needed. Measure from corner to corner to make sure that you are equal and recheck your squareness and adjust stakes as needed.

Once your deck and stair area is square, add 3' to your outer stair stakes for your landing area, which will be a concrete slab. This slab will also extend inward for 18" from the innermost point of your stair stringers. Pound in 2 additional stakes at the inward edge of your slab area. Also, extend the sides of your proposed stairs out an additional 6" on both sides of your inner and outer stakes. Adjust your stakes as needed. String this area for your slab, about 6" above the ground. Take your T-Square and make sure that the slab area and proposed stair area are square. Adjust your stakes as needed.

After completing all of the above tasks, you will need to remove any plants within your string areas. You will be removing the grass a little later.

Chapter 5: <u>**Apply for Your Permits**</u>

The best advice that I can give you about this part of the project is to put your happy face on, be polite and respectful. Dealing with the people in your town or city's Community Development Center should be an easy experience if you proceed in this manner. Remember, these are the people that will be coming out to do the various inspections required at different stages in your projects, so making them angry at the get go will only hurt you in the long run. There is no use to arguing about the various requirements. The law is the law. However, do not be afraid to question anything that you do not understand, but do it respectfully.

Go down to your town or city Community Development Center and tell them in detail of your proposed projects. They will inform you of exactly what they need, which will probably be a plot survey of your property, along with several sketches of your proposed projects. They may also ask for a couple of pictures.

This is an important step that should not be avoided. I know, that no one likes to hand out additional money just for permits for a project that they intend to do, but not doing so could cause you to either have to pay additional money (usually double the cost of the original permits) or remove the non-permitted project if you are caught. Bite the bullet and comply.

Your town or city should not only supply you with the permit applications, but also a Mission Statement outlining the specifications for certain parts of your projects that are required. These will be things like: railing height, hand rail requirements, spindle spacing, concrete slab requirements, door U-Value requirements, etc. You will need to incorporate all of these requirements into your plans.

Your plot of survey should be with your financing papers for your home loan. If you cannot locate this, you can check with the County to see if they can provide you with one. If for some reason they cannot, talk to your Community Development officials to find out what you can do.

Getting your permits approved may take a couple of weeks, so be patient. You can use that time to search for your needed materials and get the best price. Once you have all of your permits in hand, you can proceed with ordering your materials and start your projects. Be aware of the point in each part of your project where the next inspection should take place. This will help you avoid the unpleasantness of having to tear apart part of your projects in order to get the next inspection done at the proper time.

Chapter 6: <u>Installing the Access Door</u>

Existing Window - Proposed Access Door

Access Door

Access Door

Now that you have all of your permits in hand, display them as required and begin your projects by shopping for your access doors. These can be a sliding patio door or a set of French doors, whichever you prefer. You can do a search online and pick out a couple that you like, and then, go to the store and visually check them out. Be aware of the U-Value rating required by your permit. Once you find the doors that you want, purchase them, and either pick them up yourself or have them delivered.

Installing an access door can be a daunting project for anyone that has not done this before, but I assure you, you can do it. If you are just not comfortable with this part of the project, you can always hire a contractor or handyman to do it for you. However, all handymen are not created equal. I hired one to install a front door for me once, because I was uncomfortable trying it myself for my first time. The man was here working for 14 hours straight and still did not do it exactly right. It cost me about $300.00, and that was 30 years age. So, when it was time for me to install the access door for my deck, I got a video, watched it several times, and finally installed my access doors in 8 hours and it came out perfect. So, I recommend that you give it a try. Nowadays, there are numerous videos on You Tube which can walk you through the process step-by-step. I will do the same here.

First, I will give you a list of tools and supplies that you will need:

Roll of painter's tape (any size)

Claw Hammer

Corner Square (2' long or longer)

Drill

1/2" hole saw drill bit at least 6" long

Drill equal to or slightly smaller than 2 1/2" screw shank

Bit for 2 1/2" screws

Nail Set

1# box of 2" finishing nails

Wallboard Hand Saw

4' level

2 1/2" wood screws

Sawsall with long blade

Insulation

Wallboard

1# box of 1 5/8" wallboard screws

Foam Insulation

Silicone Caulk

Primer

Paint

Wallboard Tape

Wallboard Joint Compound

Bucket

Wet Sanding Sponge

Once you have your doors at your home, check the paperwork that came with them or the sticker on the door. It should tell you what your rough opening size should be. Confirm this by measuring the length and width of your doors (including your threshold) and adding 1/2" to your measurements. I will now give you instructions for installing your doors with and without an existing header.

If you are replacing an existing window that is **<u>at least as wide as your door width rough opening</u>**, perfect. You will already have a header in place. Proceed as follows:

1. Take your stud finder and confirm that you have a header in place. Mark where your header stops on the bottom end with pieces of painter's tape on both sides.

2. Now, take your stud finder and find the 2" x 4"s that are closest to the ends of your header on both sides. Mark the inside ends of these with painter's tape as well.

3. Now, check that your rough opening for your doors will fit inside of these tape marks. Check the height and the width. If they do, then proceed. If not, see the instructions for installing your doors without a header (below) and proceed as needed.

4. Measure from your floor to the top for your door rough height size and width where your proposed doors will go. Mark these with small pieces of painter's tape.

   If the window is larger than your rough opening width (as ours was) you will need to equally space your door rough opening from the existing 2" x 4"s. Mark your rough opening on all sides with your painter's tape. You will need to add 3" to each side of your rough opening for the installation of 2 - 2" x 4"s ('Jack' studs) on both sides. Move your painter's tape if necessary to add the 3" to each side.

5. Now, take your corner square and pencil and mark your top and sides at both upper corners where your painter's tape is. Then, take your 4' level and extend your lines width wise until they meet and length wise to the bottom of the proposed door (which should be to the top of your existing floor).

6. Remove your existing window.

7. Take your drill and 1/2" drill bit and drill a hole in both top corners inside your marks for your rough opening. You should drill completely through the outside of your home.

8. Now take your Sawsall with long blade and cut out your rough opening on top (even with the bottom of your header) and on both sides to the floor. Be careful not to damage your floor.

9. Remove the existing wallboard and other boards from inside your rough opening.

10. Check the height of your rough opening. If it is larger than needed, add whatever size board that you need to the bottom of your header.

11. Add your 'Jack' studs if needed to your sides, leaving enough room for your rough opening dimension. Predrill your holes before screwing your studs into your header and floor joist with your 2 1/2" screws. Make sure that you countersink your screws. Also, add any needed fiber board and tar paper on the outside, using 1 1/2" roofing nails and sliding the new tar paper under the old on top to create a water shedding effect. Cut your tar paper about 2" wider on the outside and top edge to allow for underlap. You may need to use your pry bar to pry your siding away from the wall in order for you to properly underlap your tar paper. Once you are finished, nail your siding back into place.

12. Then, you need to apply a seal to the outside of your framework using your 4" x 75' flashing

membrane tape. Apply the seal to the sides first. Measure each side, using about a 2" overlap on to your top board. Cut your membrane to length using scissors or your Stanley knife (cut on concrete or use a scrap board). Peel the top end of the backing tape for about 4" from the end. Start your membrane tape with about a 2" overlap on your top board and even with the inside edge. Press it firmly into place, especially in the corner. Then, continue to peel your tape and press your membrane to your jam as you go. Cut any excess off of the bottom. Once the inside has been firmly pressed into place, take your Stanley knife and cut the overlap in the corner at a 45 degree angle, pressing the side around the edge first and then overlap the top. Continue to press your overlapping side into place from top to bottom, trying hard to avoid any creases. Once both of your sides are done, do the same with your top, cutting your membrane tape with about a 2" overlap on each end.

13. Now, install your doors into your opening. You should have a helper outside on a ladder making sure that your doors do not fall out.

14. Square your door up on top and both sides. Check for level top and sides. Use shims to hold your door in place, making sure that you are even with the inside and outside walls. Recheck for level before screwing your doors in place. Predrill holes on both sides and top, using 3 screws for each. Drill your holes in the center of each side and top; drilling one in the center and one in each end about 3" from the corner. Use a drill bit that is slightly smaller than the shank on your 2 1/2" screw. Do not overtighten your screws. Just bring them flush with the door jam. Make sure that your doors open and/or swing properly without binding. Adjust your screws as needed. Once your door is screwed into place and you have checked it for any binding, score your shims even with your framework and take your 4" chisel and snap off any extension.

15. Add any needed insulation, along with expandable foam where appropriate. Then, cut and install any needed wallboard. You will tape and plaster this later.

16. Cut and prime your outside trim boards and install. Caulk where needed. Paint your trim boards.

17. Cut, prime, paint or stain, and install your inside trim boards. Predrill for nails and set your nail heads slightly below the surface.

18. Finish off your inside wallboard, tape, mud, sand and prime and paint as needed. Your new access door is now installed.

The following are instructions if you need to install a header. Proceed as follows:

If you need to install a 2" x 10" header above your new proposed door, you will need to cut out more of your wallboard in order for you to install your header. The header will need to be installed between 2 - 2" x 4"s, side-by-side called 'Jack' studs under your header. The space between these 'Jack' studs (inside to inside) will need to be equal to your door width rough opening. Cut out additional wallboard on your sides as needed. Make sure that you predrill your holes before screwing your studs in and countersink your screws. Use your 2 1/2" screws.

1. Measure from your floor to the top for your door's rough height size and measure the rough width where your proposed doors will go. Mark these with small pieces of painter's tape.

2. Next, take your T-Square and mark off the corners for height and width with a pencil, and take a straight edge (4' level) and pencil mark your proposed door rough opening on both sides and top.

3. Remove any existing window.

4. Take your drill and 1/2" drill bit and drill a hole in both top corners inside your marks for your rough opening, as well as, your bottom corners. You should drill completely through the outside of your home.

5. Now take your Sawsall with long blade and cut out your rough opening on top, on both sides to the floor, and along your floor. Be careful not to damage your floor. Remove all of the boards and insulation inside your opening.

6. Add the width of your header (10") to your top and mark these with pieces of painter's tape as well.

7. Using your stud finder, locate the 2" x 4"s that are closest to your outside rough opening. Mark the inside ends with painter's tape at the top, middle, and bottom of each 2" x 4". Then, pencil mark the top and sides of your proposed header, as well as, the inside of your 2" x 4"s. You will be cutting out this wallboard, but not your outside siding to this size.

8. Take your drill and drill through your <u>wallboard only</u> at the top 2 corners for your header. Take your Wallboard Hand Saw and cut out the wallboard for your header along the marked lines. Also, cut along the inside edge of both of your 2" x 4"s. Remove the wallboard.

9. Install your 2" x 10" header between the 2" x 4"s predrilling and installing 2 1/2" screws, making sure to countersink them. Then install your 'Jack' studs on either side, paying close attention to your rough opening size.

10. Go to Step 12 in the instructions for installing doors with a header already in place and complete to the end.

Now that your access doors are in, it is time to start on your deck.

Chapter 7: <u>Ordering Your Materials</u>

Now, it is time to order your materials. You will need to go through your spreadsheet and recheck price and availability. Then, decide if you will have your materials delivered or you will choose and pick up yourself.

Make sure that you have a staging area for all of the material (we had a 20' x 14' patio nearby). It is not recommended that you stage your materials in the lawn, as they will be there for a couple of weeks, which would cause your grass to die. If you do not have an ample patio, then stage everything on your driveway. Make sure that you keep it all covered with a tarp until you install it. Otherwise, the wood may start drying out and warp.

Also, make sure that you stage everything in the order that you will need it in. Go over the project in your mind so that you have easier access to the wood that you will need next.

Begin with what will be needed first, which will be your concrete and your tubes for your posts and stair slab, your 1" x 8" for your slab framing, and your limestone screening.

Post Holes

Scraped Up Sod

Scraping Up the Sod

Before you begin removing your grass, you will need to extend the perimeter of your deck an additional 8" on all sides. This will allow for your concrete pillars for your posts, as well as, the 4" x 8" bricks that you will use on your perimeter. Do not remove your existing stakes and string line, but add an additional set of stakes and string line (about 4" - 6" above the ground.

Your next task will be to take your flat spade and punch down along the perimeter of your outside string line at least 3" deep. Now, temporarily remove the inner string line. Do not remove your stakes. Once this is done, you should rent a sod cutter and remove all of the sod in your deck, stair, and slab areas.

You should find a rental place close to you that delivers and picks up the sod cutter, as the machines are extremely heavy; too heavy to lift into a pickup truck. Although you could rent ramps if you are so inclined to do so.

Once you get the sod cutter at your home, start it up and drive it to the area where the sod will be removed. Shut the machine off and set your depth to between 1/2" and 1" deep. Restart the machine and cut a row along the perimeter first. Then, cut in rows, back and forth, until all of the area has been cut. Use your flat spade to get close to your stakes.

Clean the machine, replace the gas, and call the rental place to have it picked up or deliver it.

Now, comes the fun part: picking all of the sod up and bagging it. You may need to take your flat spade and scrape up any areas that you may have missed. If you want, you can knock off any access dirt before you bag in order to make the bags lighter. If you do this, do it in your wheel barrow so that you can dump it where needed.

Once the sod has been removed, it is time to get your rototiller and till up the area under the deck and stairs to a depth of 2" and the area for your concrete slab to a depth of 8". The 2" depth is for the addition of pea gravel for under the deck, and the 8" depth for the slab will allow for 4" of crushed limestone screening for the base and 4" of concrete for the slab.

Then, take your rake and rake the dirt into piles and remove it with your shovel and wheel barrow. Dump it where needed or dump it in your driveway close to the street and tell the neighbors "Free dirt" or put up a sign. Someone will probably take it. If not, you will need to call a hauling company in order to have it hauled away.

Digging the Holes for Your Post Pillars

The first thing that you should do is restring your inner stakes. Make sure that your string line is on the outside of your stakes and taught. Now, measure out 8' from your stakes at the house along your string line and pound in stakes at these two points. Also, measure out 8' from your outside corner to the middle of your outside string line (8') and pound in another stake with the outside edge of the stake just touching the string line.

Then, you need to measure from the center of each of your middle and outside stakes (measure from the outer edge in the center of each stake) a measurement of 2 3/4" toward the center of your deck. Mark each one with a screwdriver even with the center of your stake. Do this for all 5 stakes. Then, take your other screwdriver and cut a groove in the dirt that is 6" from your center screwdriver, all the way around in a circle. Next, take your marking paint and paint each groove. These are the marks for your 12" holes for your post pillars.

Then, from the stake marking the edge of your stairs that is closest to the middle of your deck, measure from the center of the outside of that stake toward the house, 1 3/4", and place your screwdriver in at that mark. Next, measure 5" from the center in a circle around that screwdriver, scoring the dirt in the same way that you did before. Mark the groove with your marking paint. This will be a 10" wide hole which will hold a 2" x 4" post for your stairs (your 6th post).

Now that your holes are marked, temporarily take down your inner string line. You can either rent a two-man gas powered hole auger or dig the holes by hand with a post hole digger; your choice. If you use a gas powered auger, make sure that it will go 40" deep, picking it up and out of the hole that you are working on, every 4" - 6" to clear the dirt. Keep the auger running when you do this.

If you are digging the holes by hand with a post hole digger, when you reach a depth of 40" you may need to shave your sides with your curved spade in order to accept your hole tubes. When each hole has been dug, insert a hole tube to make sure that it slides down to the bottom. Adjust your sides and depth as needed to maintain a depth of at least 40" (40" + 2" for dirt already removed, for a total of 42"). This is the recommended frost line depth for your holes.

Once the holes are all dug, shovel up your dirt and place where needed.

Levelling Your Posts

You want your posts to stick out above your ground by about 6", so your tubes will need to be cut. If you are level between all of your posts (check the ground with your 4' level) than all that you need to do is to measure 8" from the ground (6" + 2" for your pea gravel) around your posts and make several pencil marks around the perimeter. Connect your marks to make a continuous circle around each post. Then, take your handsaw and follow the line, cutting each post to size. When you finish cutting each tube, place the cut end into the hole first. Check the top of each tube to make sure it is level. Adjust the bottom of your hole if necessary. Fill in any gaps around your tubes with dirt.

If your ground is not level, you will need to stack up 5 - 2" x 4"s (7 1/2") 10' long along one end of 2 of your posts. Place your 4' level in the middle and using your shims, shim up the low end until you are level. Than pencil mark each of the 2 tubes. Then, measure from the end of each tube to the mark and pencil mark the tube all the way around at the same measurement. Connect the marks and cut the tube with your hand saw. Repeat the process for all of the tubes. When you finish cutting each tube, place the cut end into the hole first. Check the top of each tube to make sure it is level. Adjust the bottom of your hole if necessary. Fill in any gaps around your tubes with dirt.

Frame Out For Your Slab

Cut 1" x 8" boards to edge out the area for your slab. Screw the boards together, predrilling your holes before screwing. Place your frame into the hole for your slab. Your frame should be 2" above the ground around it and level side to side, with a slight pitch from your proposed stairs to the opposite end. You can build up under your frame with dirt if needed. Drive a 12" stake into the ground to a depth of just below the top of your frame on each end of each side of the frame. Screw the frame from the inside into each stake using 1 5/8" wallboard screws. Pencil mark your frame (on the inside) on all (4) sides at 4" from the top.

Then, place limestone screening 2" deep into your dug out proposed slab area. Place cardboard over your screening before you tamp. Tamp down with your hand tamper.

Remove the cardboard and add an additional 2" of screening. Replace the cardboard and tamp again.

Finally, add additional screening to cover your marks by about 1/4" and do a final tamping. You are now ready for concrete.

Chapter 9: <u>Pouring Your Concrete</u>

Crew Pouring Concrete for Post Pillars & Slab

Steve, Devon, Jim, and myself.

Post Pillars & Slab Poured

Concrete Slab

Now, hook up your garden hose with a spray nozzle attached and turn on your water. Get your wheel barrow and place 7 bags of concrete near each hole. Place the remainder of your bags near your proposed slab area.

Place 2 bags into your wheel barrow. Cut the bags open by stabbing the center with your flat spade and pour the bags out into your wheel barrow. With your short handled shovel, scoop out the middle of your mixture and pile it around the center. Add about 1/4 gallon of water into the center hole of your mixture and begin mixing the dry mix with the water. Add additional water and continue to mix until mixture is completely mixed and somewhat pasty (not real soupy). If you accidentally add too much water and your mix is too runny, open a 3rd bag and mix in a little dry mix until the consistency is right.

Then, shovel the mixture into your 1st tube. Continue the process, mixing 2 bags at a time and filling the tube until full to the top. After installing each 2 bag mixture, take your curved spade and stab at the mixture fairly deep a half dozen times or so to make sure that there are no air bubbles. Then, go on to the next tube, repeating the process until all of the tubes are filled to the top.

Now go back to your 1st tube and using your concrete float, smooth the top. Repeat the process for all of your tubes. After about 30 minutes to 1 hour, take your 1/2" J - bolts and force them in to the center of each of your concrete tubes. You should check for center with your tape measure. Make sure that the threads are sticking out of the concrete about 3/4" and are straight up and down. You may need to continuously adjust the height of each of these until the concrete begins to harden. You may also need to add a little concrete to the top of each tube to maintain the height, as the concrete will tend to shrink a little as it dries. Check your bolts every 30 minutes or so and adjust as needed until the concrete begins to harden enough that they are no longer sinking.

Now that your tubes are full, continue mixing 2 bags at a time and begin filling in for your concrete stair slab. If the concrete that has been mixed and poured begins to dry out too fast before you get the next batch mixed, sprinkle it with your hose to keep it wet before adding the next 2 bag mixture. Be sure to take your shovel and stab at the poured mixture each time before pouring the next mix to make sure that there are no air bubbles. Continue filling up for the slab until you are topped off. Then, take your screed board and lay it on top of your frame at one end, and slide the screed board back and forth, pulling it along the mixture at the same time. If you begin collecting too much extra concrete as your screed, remove some with your shovel. Keep the area filled to the top and as level as possible.

After about 45 minutes, take your concrete trowel and lightly smooth out the entire surface. Use very light pressure, wetting your trowel each time before you use it. Keep an eye on your slab area every 30 minutes or so for any changes in the surface area and/or air bubbles. Add small amounts of concrete as needed to fill in for any shrinkage. Rescreed and retrowel as needed.

If for any reason, a storm comes up, you should cover all of your concrete with plastic. Place heavy bricks or boards on the outside to keep it from blowing away. Once you are finished cleaning up your concrete tools with water, call for an inspection of your pour.

Chapter 10: <u>Putting Up Your Ledger Board</u>

Ledger Board with Drip Edge

<u>Installing the Ledger Board</u>

Now with the prep work completed, your tubes are poured for your posts, as well as your stair slab, it is time to start building the deck. You will begin with the ledger board that attaches to the house.

First, measure each side out 1/4" past your vertical marks. You will cut out slightly wider than needed to allow for easier installation of your ledger board. Get your skill saw, and set your depth to about 1/2" deep. Start your saw above your top chalk line and about 1' from the end of your proposed cut. Holding the saw firmly with the front end against the board and your blade about 1" above the board, with the saw running, slowly sink the blade into the board until the saw is completely flat against the board. Then, back the saw up to the beginning of your line (do not go past it) and then move the saw forward to complete the first cut. Stop the saw before removing it from the cut.

Repeat the process for the second horizontal cut. Then, repeat the process for the 2 vertical cuts. Touch up the corners with your small wallboard hand saw and remove the board.

Now, you need to install any needed fiber board and tar paper, making sure to underlap on top and overlap on bottom for at least 2" to allow for water shedding, and overlapping or underlapping each of your sides about 2". You can use your chisel to slide the tar paper underneath where needed.

Then, take your 12" wide x 25' roll of membrane and cut it to length to cover your opening plus 2" on each side for overlap. Begin peeling back your backing paper for about 12" on one end and have your helper hold the other end taught. Overlapping your opening about 2" on the side and about 1" - 1 1/2" on top, using your putty knife to slide the membrane behind your siding board on the side, as well as, the top and bottom. Now, slowly peel and firmly stick your membrane to your tar paper, avoiding any wrinkles. Continue to the end, overlapping as needed.

Each day from now until all of your board cutting is done, if you are doing your cutting in the grass, it is best to lay out a 12' x 14' or larger tarp on the grass under your cutting area. It will make cleanup each day much easier. Now, take your 16' 2" x 10" ledger board and measure it to confirm that it is exactly 16' long. If not, set it on your saw horses and cut to size with your skill saw, setting the depth on your saw to about 1". Then, leaving it on your saw horses, measure from one end and pencil mark 3/4" from the end, and continue to make marks every 16" to mark the center of your joists. Make your marks from each end toward the center. The center joist will need to line up with your center posts, so there is no need to mark this one for now.

Then, take your joist hangers and pinch the sides together and place the center of your hanger on each of the marks and draw an outline. These marks will be where your joists will eventually go.

Now, take your 4 1/2" ledger lok screws, cordless drill, and ledger lok bit and place them near one end of where your ledger will be installed. Also, place your 4' level in the center of where the ledger will be installed.

With your helper holding one end of the ledger board and a second helper on the other, place it tight under your access door threshold and evenly spaced between the ends of your cut siding. You should have about 1/4" space on both sides. You check for level in the center of the board with your 4' level. When you are satisfied, take your drill with the bit installed and screw in a ledger lok screw at 2" from the top and 3" in from the end. Only screw it in until the washer surround makes contact with the wood. Do not countersink it. Take a second one and screw it halfway into the other end at the same measurements.

The spacing for the ledger lok screws is 6" on center, using a 'W' pattern, keeping them 2" from top and bottom. So, measure from your 1st ledger lok screw every 12" for your top row, and make an 'X' on your ledger board, keeping the marks 2" from the top. Then, measure 2" from the bottom and place an 'X' in between your marks of your top row for your bottom row of screws. Any screws that fall in the area of your joist hangers should be moved toward the previous screw mark so that you are closer spaced rather than further apart. See the 2 photos below:

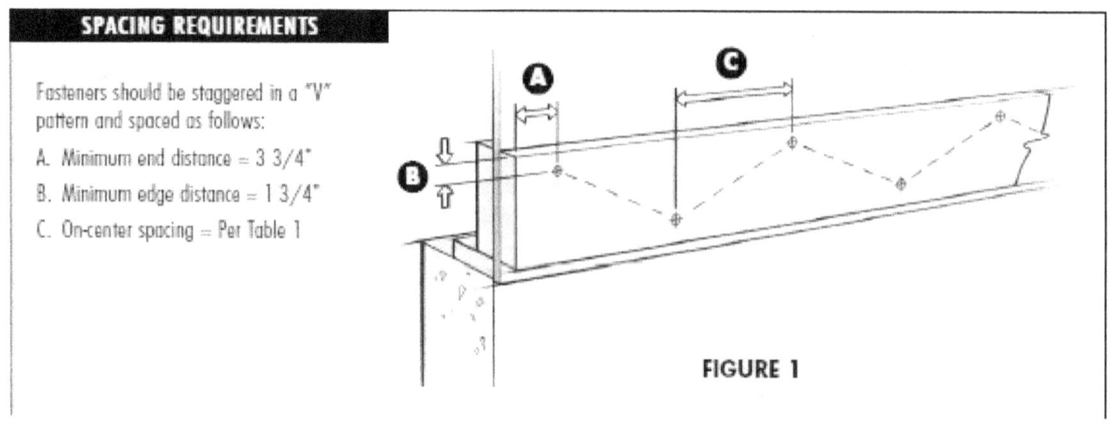

Determine the proper spacing of LedgerLOK fasteners from Table 1 below based on:

- Live load requirement for your local code
- Ledger material being attached to the house
- Rim material that you are attaching to
- Joist span as measured from the ledger to the first supporting beam

TABLE 1: Fastening pattern for attachment of ledger to rim board using LedgerLOK

Live Load	Ledger Material	Rim Material	Spacing between fasteners (in inches) based on Joist Spans of:						
			6' or Less	Up to 8'	Up to 10'	Up to 12'	Up to 14'	Up to 16'	Up to 18'
40 psf	Doug. Fir or S. Pine	2x Lumber	24	18	14	12	10	9	8
		EW Rim	25	19	15	12	10	9	8
	Hem Fir	2x Lumber	20	15	12	10	8	7	6
		EW Rim	25	19	15	12	10	9	8
60 psf	Doug. Fir or S. Pine	2x Lumber	17	13	10	8	7	6	5
		EW Rim	18	13	10	9	7	6	6
	Hem Fir	2x Lumber	14	11	8	7	6	5	4
		EW Rim	18	13	10	9	7	6	6

LedgerLOK fastening patterns outlined in this table provide equal or better performance to lag screw patterns in the 2009 and 2012 IRC in accordance with IRC sections R104.11 and in accordance with generally accepted engineering practice. Design values used to create these patterns were derived from individual fastener testing under ICC Acceptance Criteria AC233 (ESR #1078) as well as full system testing directly comparing lag screw and LedgerLOK performance in ledger to rim connections using generally accepted industry standards used to generate the IRC fastener spacing tables for lag screws.

- **Ledger materials** must be a minimum of 2 x 8 nominal dimensional pressure-preservative-treated No. 2 lumber from any of the following species: Hem-Fir, SPF, Douglas Fir or Southern Pine.

- **Rim joist materials** must be either solid sawn 2x lumber or engineered wood specifically designated by the manufacturer as rim material. 2x lumber may be of any species greater than 0.42 specific gravity, including SPF, HF or DF. Engineered Wood (EW) Rim may be OSB, LSL or LVL material measuring 1" or greater in thickness.

- **Sheating** of 15/32" or 7/16" OSB may separate the ledger and rim but must be attached per code. For additional materials between ledger and rim, please refer to the guidelines below.

Now, with a helper holding the far end of your ledger board (the end with the screw 1/2 way in, make a mark where your board is on your siding, and remove the screw while your helper holds the board in place. Then, go back to your 1st screw which has been completely installed, and continue screwing your ledger lok screws in on each one of your 'X' marks, one at a time toward the end of the board that your helper is holding. Again, be sure not to countersink any of the screws. They should be installed flush only. Doing things this way will insure that your ledger sits perfectly flat against your house with no gapping in the center.

Installing the Drip Edge

Now that your ledger board is in place, it is time to install a drip edge on top of it. Take your 1st piece of 10' aluminum white flashing and some of your 1 1/2" galvanized nails and install the flashing on top of your ledger board. Trim the flashing as needed with your tin snips so that it fits between your access door threshold and your ledger board. Slide the rest under your siding as needed. You will need to predrill holes for your nails to be installed; using a bit that is equal to or slightly smaller than your nail shank.

Then, overlapping your 1st piece of flashing for at least 2", cut the 2nd piece of flashing to the correct length, leaving room to slide it behind the edge of your siding for at least 2". Then, trim the flashing as needed and install it with the overlap. Next, take your 4" flashing tape, and cover the flashing completely. When finished, take a tube of your silicone caulk and caulk the top of the flashing to your threshold, and along the sides and below your ledger board to the house siding. You should cut the tip of your caulk tube at a 45 degree angle, about 1/2" from the tip. Then, poke the tube with your long, thin rod to break the seal. Install the tube in your caulk gun with the cut end pointing down and pull the trigger until the caulk begins to flow.

After that, go ahead and caulk around your outside door trim.

Chapter 11: <u>Install Your Posts & Add Rim Joists</u>

Posts, Rim Joists, and Center Cross Beam

<u>Install Post Anchors</u>

The first thing that you need to do now is to install your 6" x 6" post anchors with cover tops and your 4" x 4" post anchor with cover top. Place each post anchor over the bolt in the pillar, place a flat washer, lock washer, and nut on each bolt and lightly snug them down (not totally tight). You need to be able to hit them with your rubber mallet and move them around slightly. Place your upright wings (nail plates) toward the sides of your deck, with the 3/8" hole for your lag bolt toward the outside.

<u>Adjust Anchors and Cut Posts</u>

Then, place your cover top on each post anchor. If they do not sit flat without wobbling, then your bolt is a little too long. You will need to trim your bolt down a little with a hacksaw. Only take a few threads off at a time until your top plate sits flat. Once you have installed the washers, nuts, and tops on all of your post anchors, you need to take your 6" x 6" x 10' posts and cut them in half with your chain saw. You also need to cut 1 of your 4" x 4" x 8' posts down to 5' long. Do this on your saw horses, clamping your wood to your saw horses with your adjustable clamps. Make sure that your chain saw is filled with gas mixture (if it is gas powered) and make sure that it is filled with chain saw oil.

Cut Notches in Your 1st Post

Now you will need to determine if your posts will need to be notched out or not in order to accept your rim joists. This will be determined by the accuracy of your placing your J-Hook anchor bolts in the center of your post. Some of our posts required notching and some did not. You will check this as follows:

Then, take your 1st 6" x 6" post and stand it up in the center post hanger on one side of your proposed deck. Put the end that was not cut, down. This will make it more stable. Do the same with your outside corner post on the same side.

Now, with a helper on each end, run a string line even with the top and end of your ledger board to the outside top end of your post. This string line represents the outside face of your rim joist. Check the line for level with a line level. Also, check for square where your line meets your ledger board. Once level and square, see where your line lines up with your posts. Adjust your posts to get them as close to the line as possible. This will tell you if either or both posts need to be notched out or not. If you can get your posts to touch your string, you will need to notch them out. If not, see if you can adjust them 1 1/2" away from your string. In this case, they will not need to be notched. Mark any post that needs to be notched. Then, do the same on the other side of your ledger board for your other two outside posts.

With a helper on either end of your string line, level your line with the line level (forget about being square to your ledger board for now). Now, pencil mark where your line crosses each post. This is where your posts will need to be cut. Then, measure the width of your rim joist and transfer that measurement from the top mark on your post toward the ground for the post closest to the house. Do the same for your outside post, only if it needs to be notched.

Then, the post closest to the house will need to also be notched out for your cross beam. Remember, your other joists (excluding your rim joists) are only 2" x 8"s, so there will be 2" variance that you need to deal with. You will take the width of your cross beam boards, and transfer that measurement beginning 2" above the lower of your 1st two marks and downward (in order to compensate for the 2" variance), placing the marks on the side of your post that faces the house. Measure the width of your 2" x 8"s in order to make sure that the 2" variance is correct. Make any adjustment needed. Take your small T-Square, and make all of your marks on both post faces go from end to end.

Then, place the post closest to the house on to your saw horses, and using your chain saw, cut the post down to just below your top mark on the post. Now, if you are notching the post, take your skill saw, set the depth to **1 1/2" deep**, and beginning with your lower mark, cut slots completely across the post. Space your slots about **1/8" apart**, continuing to cut until you reach the top of your post.

Now, take your 4" heavy duty chisel, place it in between 2 cuts about 1/3 of the way from the end and force your chisel to snap off the pieces. Continue doing this with the remainder of the cuts, removing all of the pieces. Then, take your hammer and chisel, holding the chisel at about a 45 degree angle and holding it lightly so as to not gouge into the post, chisel off any remainder of your slots until the area is fairly smooth.

Once you notch your 1st post if needed, flip your post 90 degrees so that the marks for your center beam are facing up. Then, set your saw to a depth of **3"** (or as close as you can get it). Repeat the notching cutting process

<u>**but do not remove them yet**</u>. When you are finished, flip your post 90 degrees and measure 3" in from the top and bottom of your marks from the outside edge of your post toward the center. Connect the marks. Then, take you skill saw and carefully make a cut along that mark, keeping your saw perpendicular to your post. Next, flip your post 180 degrees and repeat the process for the other side. Now, flip your post with the notches facing up and remove all of your notch. Use your Sawsall to touch up any area of your notch that needs it. Once you have cleaned up the bottom of your notch with your chisel and Sawsall, check it on both ends for a depth of 3". Touch up as necessary, and return the post to the anchor, placing the non-cut end down. Place the post with the lower (cross beam) notch facing the house.

<u>Repeat the Process for Corner Post on That Side</u>

Now, repeat the process for the corner post on that side, except you will not have a notch cut for a beam. Depending on the amount of adjustment in your corner post anchor will determine whether or not you can cut an additional notch for your tail rim joist. We will check this later, after we have done the rim joist on the other side.

Then, set the posts back into your anchors with the non-cut end facing down. Then, take your rim joist and place it against the end of your ledger board and even on the top. Adjust your posts to meet it, putting it inside any notches. Using your corner square, square the rim joist to the ledger board and adjust your posts as needed. Next, set the rim joist down, remove your center post and tighten the anchor tight. Replace the top cap and post (making sure that your notches are on the correct sides), center it within the anchor, use your post level to level the post and then nail the anchor to the post using your 1 1/2" galvanized nails. Nail in all of the holes. You will not be securing your outer post at this time.

Now, go ahead and place the rim joist back into place, square and level it, clamp it to your posts, and install your corner brace on the inside corner of where your ledger board meets your rim joist. Nail it in using 1 1/2" galvanized nails, nailing it into the ledger board first, then, lining up the top of the rim joist even with the top of the ledger board, and nailing the corner brace into the rim joist. Be sure to use nails in all of the holes.

Then, level and secure the rim joist to the center post with your 2 - 2 1/2" screws. Place your screws in the center of the post about 2" from the top and bottom of your rim joist. You can also temporarily screw the rim joist to the outer post in the same manner. You will need to remove these later in order to properly align your outer posts.

Then, repeat the entire process for the other rim joist (the other side of your deck).

Next, you will need to remove the screws from both rim joists that are screwed into your outer posts. Then, take a string line between your outer corners and adjust your 3 outer posts as needed in order to determine if any will be notched out.

Notch any posts that are necessary, replace, level, remove posts, tighten anchors, and replace posts. Now, mark and cut the ends of your rim joists appropriately. Then, secure the tail rim joist to your posts by first clamping it to your post, checking for level, and then, using 2 1/2" screws as you did before.

Next, you will need to secure the joists to the posts using bolts. For your center post, make a mark for your top bolt at 2" from the top and centered between the edge of your post and the center of the post. Your bottom mark will be 2" from the bottom of your joist and centered on the other side of your post center. Clamp your rim joist securely to your post. Double check your joist and post for level. Using your 1/2" hole saw and electric drill, drill your holes through your joist and your post, being careful to keep your drill level while drilling.

Now, place a flat washer on each of your 2 bolts, put them into the holes, place another flat washer, lock washer, and lock nut on each bolt and tighten down until the washers are sunk slightly into the wood.

Next, your outside corner post will have 4 bolts installed, 2 from the side and 2 from the rear, so the hole pattern will be a little different.

So, mark the spots for the side rim joist as follows: your top bolt will be 2" from the top and centered between the edge of your post and the center of your post as before, but your bottom bolt, while still centered between the center of your post and the other end, it will be 4" from the bottom. This pattern will allow the bolts that will hold your tail rim joist to be 4" from the top and 2" from the bottom.

Clamp your joist to your post. Drill your holes and install and tighten your bolts as before. Repeat the process for the other side of the deck.

You will not be notching your 4" x 4" post for your stairs. This will be attached flush with your rim joist. You will cut the top of this post even with your joist and secure the post anchor in the same manner. Level the post with your post level, clamp your joist to your post, drill your 2 holes, and secure with bolts as you did for your other posts. You will be cutting the notch for your center posts and securing them at a later time. You will also be installing your cross beam after all of your joists are installed.

Notch Your Posts for Your Cross Beam

Regardless of whether or not you needed to notch your posts or not in order to accept your rim joists, you will need to notch all 3 of the center posts out in order to accept your cross beam. Your outside center posts should already be notched for your center beam. Now, it is time to mark and notch the center post that is located in the center of your deck. This notch will be cut on the side of the post that will face the house and will be 3" deep to accommodate 2 - 2" x 10" x 16' boards for your cross beam the same as your outside post notches.

Take one of the 2" x 10" x 16' boards that you will use for your cross beam, and with a helper on each end, hold the board under your outside rim joist on the far end with the outside edge even with the outside edge of your rim joist there. On the other end, mark your crossbeam where the outside edge meets the outside of the other rim joist. This cross beam will be cut to this length later.

Now, hold your cross beam with the outside edge to the inside of your rim joist on one end and with the cross beam even with your outside posts notches. Tap your center post as close to the crossbeam as possible and make a mark top and bottom where the notch will need to be cut. Set the crossbeam down.

Then, measure from your ledger board to your tail rim joist where your center joist will go, and cut a 2" x 8" joist to that length. Now, hold that board even with the top or your ledger board and tail rim joist and mark your post where the top of the joist crosses it. This will be where you will cut your post for height.

Now, remove the post, set it on your saw horses, clamp it down, and using your chain saw, cut it to length on your mark. Then, using your small T-Square, mark for your notch across the post, top and bottom from end to end. Cut your notch as you did before (3" deep), the same as you did for your outside center posts.

Do not cut separate notches in order to mount your cross beams on either side of the post. This method is incorrect. Now it is time to install the rest of your joists.

Chapter 12: <u>Install Your Joists, Weed Block & Pea Gravel</u>

Installed Pea Gravel and Perimeter Bricks

<u>Install Weed Block and Perimeter Bricks</u>

Before you install your joists, you should put down your weed block and install your perimeter bricks. You will be installing your pea gravel as you install your joists, beginning near the center and installing a couple of joists toward each end, then dumping and spreading your pea gravel. Continue with this process until it is complete.

So, if you have not had your pea gravel delivered yet, you should do so now. Installing it as you put in your joists will make it easier for you to dump it and spread it out, without having to duck all of the joists. You should place a tarp on your driveway near your garage door if possible, in order to make cleanup easier. Have your delivery dumped here.

First, you need to install your weed block. Roll out your weed block beginning at the end of your deck furthest from the house. Roll your 1st row out, cut to size, and using a hammer and your staples, place staples at the 2 furthest corners from the house first, pulling the weed block tight. Then, install additional staples about every 5' about 2" from the end.

Next, install your next row of weed block, overlapping the 1st row by 3" - 4". Staple in place the same way, installing staples through the bottom only (which will also be going through the top of your 1st row). Continue this process until the entire under the deck area has been covered.

Then, take your levelling sand and sprinkle it along the edge where your bricks will be installed. Level out the sand, making it about 1/4” - 1/2” deep. Take your rubber mallet and beginning at the house, start installing the bricks end to end, tapping them down with your mallet until each one is level with the previous. Add or remove sand as needed. If your corner does not come out even from edge to side, you can either cut the corner brick with a wet saw or extend your back line out to match the end of the brick, whichever you prefer. You can also get a masonry blade for your skill saw and dry cut the brick if you do not have a wet saw. Continue installing all of the needed bricks until complete.

Install Joists and Pea Gravel

The first thing that you should do is take your 25’ tape measure, and with a helper holding the end at the ledger board, measure from there to your tail rim joist for each joist and write down your measurements. Cut each joist to the proper length, leaving the center joist till last, begin near the center and while a helper holds each end of the joist even with the top of the ledger board and the top of the tail rim joist, place your hanger under the joist making sure that it is tight against the bottom. While your helper holds one end of the hanger against the ledger and tight against the joist, push your side of the hanger tight against the joist and install the top 1 1/2” galvanized nail into the ledger board to hold your hanger. Have your helper put the top nail in on his side as well. Then, install your galvanized nails into the rest of the hanger holes on the ledger. Then, install nails into the hanger holes to attach the hanger to the joist. Do the other end of the joist the same way. Install a couple of joists on each side of center, making sure to line up the top of your joist even with the top of your ledger and tail rim joist board, while making sure that the hanger is tight against the bottom of the joist. Be sure to put a nail in every hole in the hangers.

Once you have 2 joists on either end of center, begin dumping your pea gravel and levelling it to the top of your 2” depth. Continue the process of installing 2 joists at a time toward each outside rim joist and putting down and spreading the pea gravel. Doing it this way will make dumping the pea gravel easier.

Notch Out Your Center Post and Install the Final Joist

Now that all of your joists are in except for the center one, take your center joist (after cutting it to length) with a helper on each end and line it up tight to your center posts and the top of your ledger board and tail rim joist. Adjust your post anchor plates as needed. Then, pencil mark around your plates. Then, mark where the top and bottom of your joist is on the center post closest to the house, as well as, marks on the outside post where the top and bottom of the joist hanger will be. Then, set the joist on the ground.

Then, take out the center post closest to the house and on the side of the post that faces the house, measure from your mark (which marks the bottom of the joist) the distance of the width of your cross beam. Take the post to your saw horses, use your chain saw to cut it to length, and notch out 3” for your cross beam as you did before. Then, return the post to the post anchor, but do not nail it in yet. Set the non-cut end on the bottom.

Then, remove your outer center post, and take it to your saw horses. Using your skill saw, make a 1/8” notch between the two marks on your post from the top to the bottom mark and slightly beyond. This notch will be to compensate for the joist hanger and nail heads. The width of your notch should be just slightly wider than one side of your joist hanger. Install your final joist, making sure that it is tight against both of your center posts. Adjust your posts with a rubber mallet as needed. Install the joist hanger on the ledger first and also, nail the hanger to the joist on that end. Then, nail in the joist hanger to the tail rim joist on the side which is away from the post, making sure that the hanger is tight against the joist. Next, nail the hanger to the joist on that side. Remove your post and finish nailing the hanger to the tail rim joist and the joist.

Remove your center post closest to the house and tighten your nut on your anchor. Replace the plate top and the post, level the post with your post level, and nail it into place. Tighten the nut on your outer center post anchor, replace the top, and replace the post (non-cut end down). Level and nail into place.

Now, after predrilling, install your 2 - 2 1/2" screws holding your center joist to your center posts. Then, drill holes for your bolts and install them the same way that you did previously.

Now, take your 3/8" - 1 1/2" long lag screws and install one into each post anchor (into the 3/8" hole). Rake your pea gravel level as needed.

Chapter 13: <u>Install Your Cross Beam & Joist Braces</u>

Installed Cross Beam with Rafter Ties

<u>Install Your Cross Beam</u>

Now it is time to install your cross beam and joist braces. You will put in your cross beam first.

First, you need to measure the length from the outside edge of one rim board to the opposite outside edge. Then, cut your 2 cross beam boards to that length. Before you can install your cross beam, you will need to notch out the corners so that the beam will fit flush under your rim joists, as well as, tight against the bottom of your joists. Measure the difference between the width of your rim joist and your other joists. This is the amount that you will need to cut out from the edge of your cross beams and down, 1 1/2" from both edges on each upper corner.

Once these cuts are made (using your skill saw and sawsall), set your first beam into place, resting on the notches, lining up the edges, and using 2 - 2 1/2" screws for each post, screw your beam into place. Screw your screws in the center of the posts, about 2" from top and bottom of the beam.

Place your second beam against the first and hold it in place with your clamps. Screw the second beam into the first, avoiding your original screws. Then, in the same manner as you did for your posts, drill 2 holes through the beams and each of the posts. Bolt it all together using bolts, flat washers, lock washers, and lock nuts. Tighten securely. Then, using 2 1/2" screws, screw the 2nd beam to the 1st, using a screw every 12" top and bottom, 2" from the ends.

Install Your Rafter Tie Hardware

Now it is time to install your rafter ties, which tie in your joists to your crossbeam. Using your 1 1/2" galvanized nails, nail in your tie to your joist first. Then, with a helper standing on each joist, pull it down until your joist is touching your crossbeam. Now, nail each tie to your crossbeam. Be sure to use a nail in each and every hole.

Install Your Cross Braces

Now, using 2" x 8" boards, measure between each of your joists and cut a board to fit in between. Measure out 4' from your ledger board and install your 1st brace using 2 - 2 1/2" screws, each 2" from either end of the board. Now stagger your next brace inward (toward the center) 1 1/2". Screw into place. Continue installing braces, each one in line with the one before the previous one, so that you essentially have 2 rows aligning. Do the same 4' away from your tail rim joist. Doing this will make your deck incredibly solid.

Once you have finished your framing, call for an inspection.

Stair Stringers

It is important that all of your stairs are the same height and that they fall between 7" and 7 1/2" from the top of the step to the top of the next step. Fortunately, purchasing precut stringers usually takes care of most of the guess work (ours were at 7 1/8"). However, you will probably need to cut down the bottom a little bit. Remember, even your last step (going down) will need to be the same height from the top of the stair above it to your landing (concrete slab). You can check your height by adding 1" to your measurement of the step in your stringer (assuming you are using 5/4" boards for your steps). Measure each step in the stringer, adding 1" to the measurement. Then measure the last one (lowest one) from the concrete slab landing and add 1" to the top of the first stair. Cut the bottom of your stringers as needed.

Now, add 1" to the top step (for your deck boards), and add the 1" to the step below it. This measurement is where the top of your stringer should be (approx. 7 1/8"). Pencil mark your rim joist on each spot where the top of the stringers will go. Remember, they will be just like your joists; spaced 16" on center. Assuming that your stairs will be about 48" wide, pencil mark at the first spot (near your tail rim joist). Line up the inside edge of your stringer with the inside edge of your post. Then, make a mark at 16", 32", and 48". These marks will mark the same side of each stringer as the first. Measure down from the top of your rim joist (above the stringers) and measure down at those points, the distance of the height of your stairs. Place a cross mark on each of the 4 spots. This is where the top of your stringer needs to be. Slide your 1st stringer into a stringer hanger and place it up against your rim joist. You should notice that there is not enough wood to nail the hanger to.

So, you need to add a piece of 2" x 8" between your 4" x 4" post and your corner post and screw it into your posts directly below the rim joist. This will give you ample nailing wood for your hangers.

Now, slide your stringer (in the hanger) back up to your 1st mark, line up the top of your stringer even with the mark. Also make sure that your inside edge of the stringer is even with the inside edge of the post. Now, using your 1 1/2" galvanized nails, attach your stringer hanger to the joist piece that you just installed, as well as, to your rim joist. Be sure that the top of your stringer is level and use nails in all holes in the hanger.

Continue nailing in your other 3 stringers and hangers in the same way, checking each one for level and proper alignment before nailing it in. Then, measure the distance between your stringers at the top and the bottom (should be about 14 1/2"). Cut 6 - 2" x 10" pieces, each to the proper length. Predrill holes and screw these spacers in between your stringers in the middle of your top stair and in the middle of your bottom stair. You should place these in vertical and near the front face of your step, but not beyond. Also, the top must be below your stair. Check for level across all of your stringers with your 4' level.

Chapter 15: <u>Install Your Posts for Your Railing</u>

Posts for Railing

<u>Deck Posts</u>

Now it is time to cut and install your posts and framework for your deck and stair railing. You will be using 4" x 4" posts and 2" x 4"s for your framework.

Your railing should be a minimum of 36" high, so your posts will need to be cut in 45" lengths for most of them. We arrived at this figure as follows: 9" for most of the side of your rim joist, 1" for your deck boards, and 36" for your railing height - 1" for your top rail. Your posts for your stairs will be about 50". So you should get a deck post and a stair post out of 1 - 8', 4" x 4" post. You will need 10 posts for your deck and an additional 4 posts for your stair railing.

So, cut 10 posts at 45" and place them in one stack, and the remainder of the cut portions in another stack. You can measure and cut all of your posts at one time using your chain saw. Then, stack them where they will be convenient to access.

Now, take your 1st 45" post and cut a notch 3 1/2" from one end down. Cut the notch 1 1/2" deep. Set your skill saw to that depth before cutting the notch. You should clamp your post to your saw horse while cutting it. Remove the cut slices and place them in a 5 gallon bucket. You may need a few to use as shims in order to level your posts. Then, cut a second notch 3 1/2" wide, 1 1/2" deep, beginning at 13 1/2" and going to 17" from the other end of your post. Now, from the end of the post (of that last notch), measure 1" from the inside edge of the notch and place a pencil mark. Using your small T-Square (the 45 degree angle part), pencil mark a line from that mark at a 45 degree angle to the outside edge of your post. Cut this small corner off with your skill saw. Repeat the process for all 10 of your deck posts. This will give the bottom of your posts a little dimension and will match your balusters which will be cut in a similar fashion.

Next, take your 1st post and place it flush against one of your rim joists beginning at 2" from your house siding. Clamp your post to your rim joist near the edge on top and on the opposite side near the bottom. Level the post with your post level. If needed, use a shim (from your notch cuttings) top or bottom of your post to make it level. Once level, screw in 2 - 2 1/2" screws at 2" from top and bottom of your rim joist, at the center of your post. Then, remove the clamps, recheck your level, and when good, drill 2 holes with your 1/2" hole drill and electric drill; one hole at 2" from the top of the rim joist and in the center of the edge of your post and the center. Drill the second hole at 2" from the bottom of your post and on the other side of post center, centering the hole in between center and edge of your post. Bolt your post to your rim joist using flat washers on both inside and outside of rim joist, and lock washer and lock nut on the inside of the joist. Tighten both securely until the washers are slightly recessed into the wood. Recheck for level with your post level, both side to side and front to back. Repeat this process for your other side of your deck closest to the house.

Then, your outer 2 corners will require something a little extra. Your deck posts will be attached to your rim joists, not to your tail rim joist. Start with the post that will go to the outside edge of your stairs (assuming that you are putting your stairs near your tail rim joist). First, you will not be cutting your 2 notches in the post as you did for your other posts. You will be using 2" x 4" hangers to attach your rail supports on this post instead. You will also be cutting some notches for your stair railing supports into this post at a later time.

You will be lining up the inside edge of your post with the inside edge of your 1st stringer. Therefore, you will need to cut a notch in the post 1 1/2" wide and as high as the top of your stringer is from the existing bottom of the post minus 1/2". You will need to take the measurement from the top of your joist to the top of your stringer, and then, using this measurement, transfer it to your post and trim accordingly. Remember to deduct 1/2" from the measurement, since your post will not extend down to the top of your stringer. Cut your 45 degree trim edge at the bottom as you did before on the portion of the post that is left (longest part).

Now, you will need to place your post flat against your side rim joist and next to the top bolt head of your deck post. Pencil mark where the top and bottom of your bolt head is on your post. Then, move your post to the other side of the lower bolt and do the same thing. Now measure from the outer edge of your deck frame to the center of your top bolt, and transfer that measurement to the center of your top marks on the inside (notched end) of the post. Make an 'X' at that spot. Do the same for your lower bolt, marking your post on the inside (notched end) of the post.

Now, take your hole saw and **gently** drill to the depth equal to your bolt head (about 1/2" deep). Your post should now fit over your existing bolt heads and should be flush to your rim joist. If not, carefully drill a little deeper. Clamp your post to the rim joist, top and bottom. Level the post, using a shim if necessary, and screw the post to the rim joist. Then, taking note of where your existing bolt heads are for your 6" x 6" post, mark for your 4" x 4" bolts on the opposite side of center for both bolts (one to left of center, the other to right of center). Drill your holes with your 1/2" drill bit and install your bolts, washers, and nut. Lock down tightly. Recheck level. Adjust as needed. Then, repeat the process for the other outside corner post with the exception of putting in the stringer notch. You will cut notches in this post as you have done previously.

Now that you have your 4 corner posts installed, you will need to install 2 more posts on each rim joist and 2 more posts on your tail rim joist. Starting with your tail rim joist, measure the distance between your corner posts and divide by 3. This will be the distance between the inside edge of a corner post to the center of your next post, from the center of that post to the center of your next post, and finally, from the center of that post to the inside edge of the opposite corner post. Mark your tail rim joist for this dimension which will mark the center of your posts. If a post falls on where a joist hanger is located, you will need to move your post left or right to avoid the hanger when drilling for your bolt holes. Whichever way you move 1 post, you should move the other in the opposite direction in order to keep your spacing between your corners post and the next post as equal as possible.

Cut notches in the posts in the same way that you did your others, trim cut the lower edge, level, screw to your joist, drill your holes, level, and bolt your posts tight to your rim joist.

Now, you need to notch the other post for the stair side of your deck. You already have one post for your stairs (assuming that you are putting your stairs in near your tail rim joist). You will notch out this post the same way that you did the post on the other side of your stairs, just cutting your vertical notch for your stringer on the opposite side. Install this post as you did the others.

Then, measure from the inside of the inside stair post to the inside of the post closest to the house, and put a post in the center. Transfer the dimensions of your post locations to the other side of your deck for the posts there, so that posts on both sides are in alignment.

<u>Center and Lower Stair Posts</u>

Now you need to cut and notch the center and lower posts for your stairs. Beginning with the lower posts, cut these post to 50" in length. Then, notch them out to fit over your outside stringers. Cut your notch 1 1/2" deep and the length equal to the height of you stringer. Clamp them to either side of your stair stringers, centering them in your final step. Level both posts. Screw in 2 2 1/2" screws, one top and one bottom in the center of your post, and 2" from the top and bottom. Remove the clamp.

Drill 2 - 1/2" holes through each post and stair stringer, offsetting them and keeping them 2" from the ends of your stringers. Make sure that you avoid your spacers that are in between your stringers. Stay at least 1 1/2"f away from them. Bolt the posts to the stringers snuggly and check for level. Install a shim if needed for either or both posts. Do not completely tighten them at this time. You will be removing them in a bit in order to notch out for your railing side supports.

Now, cut your 2 center posts to 51 1/2" long, and set them in the center of your 4th stair from the top on either side of your stair stringers, lining up the bottom of the post and the stringer. Clamp them in place.

Then, mark each post where the top of the stringer stair is. Remove your clamps, and cut a 1 1/2" deep notch from the mark to the bottom of the post. 45 degree angle cut the bottom of the post, measuring along the bottom from the inside of the notch for 1", and marking your 45 degree angle from that mark to the outside of your post.

Set the post against your stringer in the center of your 4th stair from the top, clamp it to your stringer, and level with your post level. Use a shim if necessary. Once it is level, screw the post to your stringer to hold it in place while you drill your 2 - 1/2" holes for your bolts. Offset your holes as before, staying 2" from the top and bottom of your stringer. Bolt the post to the stringer, level and snug up both bolts, but do not tighten tight. Repeat the process for the post on the other side of your stairs.

Chapter 16: <u>Install Most of Your Deck Railing Supports</u>

Railing Supports

<u>Cut and Install Your Deck Railing Supports</u>

Now, it is time to cut and install your 2" x 4" railing supports for your deck. Beginning with the railing for the side of the deck opposite the stairs, measure for the top rail from the outside edge of the post closest to the house (at the bottom of your top notch) to the outside edge of your outer corner post. Subtract 1 1/2" from this measurement and cut your rail. Mount it on your posts inside of your top notch, staying flush to the outside of your post nearest your house. Clamp at each post. Drill 2 screw holes in your railing for each post, using 2 1/2" screws in each, one left of center, one right, and each about 1" from the edge. Your railing should be even or slightly above your posts. Repeat the process for you bottom rail on that side.

Now, measure for your railing for the tail end of the deck. Measure from the inside of the bottom of the top notch in your corner post (on the side where you just installed the rails) to the inside of your other corner post (the unnotched post). Cut your 2" x 4" to the proper length. Now, insert your rail into your notched corner post and your other notched posts. Clamp the rail to your 2 center posts. Predrill screw holes in the rail to attach this rail to the previously installed rail. Screw in your 2 screws. Predrill and install screws through the rail to attach to your 2 center posts. Now, take your 2" x 4" hanger, hold it under your rail, and line up the top of the rail with the top of your corner post. Take 1 1/2" galvanized nails and attach your hanger to the post. Also nail your hanger to the rail. Repeat the process for your bottom rail.

Now, go to the final side of your deck. Measure from the bottom of your top notch and from the outside of your post closest to the house to the outside edge of the post near your stairs. Subtract 1 1/2" from the measurement and cut your rail to length. Lay it on your deck, but do not install it at this time. Repeat the process for your lower rail.

Now, you will need to put up your stair risers and steps before you can complete your stair railing.

Chapter 17: <u>Install Your Stair Risers and Stairs</u>

Stair Risers & Stairs

<u>Install Your Stair Risers</u>

You will need to cap your stairs before you can finish the rails for your deck and stairs. Begin with your risers. The riser is the board that goes on the face of your stair. Measure across your stringers from end to end. It should be about 49 1/2". You will want to have your risers and stair steps overhang your stringer by about 1/2" - 3/4" on each side. So, if your boards are 49 1/2" wide, your risers should be cut to 50 1/2" - 51" long. They should all be equal. You will be using 1" x 8" for your risers. Cut all of your risers now.

Your 1st riser will need to be installed 1" above the top of your rim joist in order to cap off the ends of your deck boards. You can cut a couple of your stair step boards and lay them across your joists close to your riser to help with the measurement. Adjust your riser so that the overhang is equal on each end of your stringers. Then, drill 2 screw holes in line with the center of each stringer, 2" from the top and bottom. Using 2 1/2" screws, screw in your riser with the top of the riser even with the top of your deck board pieces. Countersink your screws about 1/8".

Lay each riser on each step and measure the overhang on each side. Adjust the board until your overhang is equal on each side. Then, drill 2 screw holes for each stringer, 2" from the top and bottom, and centered in your stringer. Using 2 1/2" screws, screw in your risers with the top of the riser even with the top of your stringer step. Countersink your screws about 1/8". Do this for all your risers.

<u>**Install Your Stair Steps**</u>

Now, using your 5/4" x 6" boards, cut all of your steps the same length as your risers. You will need 2 boards for each step. Predrill holes for your 2 1/2" screws about 2" from your riser and about 3" from the outer end of each board. Butt your 1st board tight against your riser, line it up with your riser and screw it in. Then, butt your 2nd board tight against the first and screw it in. Do this for all of your stairs.

Once you get to your center stair posts, you will need to notch out your step boards to go tight around the posts. You will do the same once your reach your bottom posts.

Chapter 18: Install Your Stair Railing and Complete Your Deck Railing

Cut and Install Your Stair Railing Supports

Before you can install your final side of deck rails, you must notch out the deck post closest to your stairs to accept your stair rails. Take a 2" x 4" that you will use for one of your lower rails and lay it on your stairs close to your posts on either side of your stairs. Have the rail extend beyond the top and bottom post. Raise your rail up about 1/2" from your stair step and clamp your rail to all 3 of your posts.

Then, take your top rail for that same side, extending it past your top and bottom posts, clamp it to the top of your post. The rail should be even with the tallest part of your post. Now, pencil mark each of your posts, top and bottom of each rail. Also mark the ends of each rail at the outside of your posts except for the top rail at the bottom post. You will extend this rail 12" beyond your bottom post. Then, take your rails down and cut each one to length and set aside. You will now need to remove each of your posts that have been marked, clamp them to your saw horses, and cut your notches in between your marks at a depth of 1 1/2". Then, reinstall your post and tighten securely, making sure that you are level. Shim if needed. Repeat this process for all 3 posts on that side. Now, repeat the process for the other side of your stairs.

Complete Your Deck Railing

Now that your stair railing supports have been cut, before you mount them, you need to complete your last section of deck supports. Measure for your top rail from the outside of the post closest to the house to the outside of the post at your stairs, deduct 1 1/2" from your measurement and cut your top rail. Mark your 2" x 4" and cut to length. Do the same for your bottom rail. Place your top rail in place and clamp to your post, with the rail even with the outside of the post closest to the house. Predrill your holes for the rail and screw into your posts as you did for your other railing supports. Then, remove your clamps and repeat the process for the bottom rail.

Install Your Stair Railings

Now that your deck railing supports have been installed, you should screw in your stair railing supports. Mount them in the same manner that you did for your deck railing supports. Make sure that the longer rails on each side of mounted on the top.

Then, you will install your top rails on your stairs. Take a 5/4" x 6" board and clamp it to your rail support near your top post. Clamp the bottom end as well. Now, mark a parallel line down the end of your rail that is parallel to your post. Take the rail down, set it on your saw horses and clamp it into place. Then, adjust your skill saw to the angle needed in order to cut your mark and make the cut.

Now, set your railing back into place and clamp it to your rail support with a 1" overhang on the inside (near your stairs). Mark the end of your rail closest to the bottom post with a 1" overhang of your rail support, and make a parallel mark which is parallel to your post. Take the rail down, adjust your skill saw to the angle and make the cut. Repeat the process for the other side of your stairs.

Now, place your rails back into place with a 1" overhang on the inside (near your stairs) and clamp to your support rails. Beginning at the top, measure down 2" from your top post and 1 3/4" from the inside edge and make a mark. Now, measure from the lower end of your rail up 3" (same measurement from the inside edge). Then, measure from your top mark to your bottom mark and divide your measurement equally so that your other marks will be about 10" - 12" apart. Make additional marks for your screws at these intervals. All marks should be 1 3/4" from the edge. Predrill your marks and screw the railing in using 2 1/2" screws, countersinking each screw about 1/8". Then, repeat the process on the other side of your stairs for your other railing.

Now, put your railings up around your deck. Beginning at the post closest to the house and with your railing overhanging the post 1" toward the house and 1" on the inside (toward your deck), make a mark at 1" past your furthest post. Cut the railing to length and install it the same way that you did your stair railing. Then, complete your railing for the other sides of your deck.

Now, you will need to install your additional hand rails for your stairs. These should be sealed with at least 2 coats of outside sealer before installing. While your hand rails are drying, using scrap pieces of your 1" x 8" riser boards, cut out 8 blocks, 3" wide and 3 1/2" long for backers for your hand rail brackets. Mount these brackets with 2 screws each, predrilling and using 1 1/2" screws. Place the screws at opposite corners about 1" from the corners. Line your outside block corner with the outside edge of your top and bottom posts. Space the other 2 blocks for each side equally between your outside blocks.

Now, with a helper holding each end of your hand rail against the edge of your railing board, mark each end at the outside edge of your top post and at the edge of your railing at the bottom. Make your marks parallel to your posts on both ends. Cut your railing. Repeat the process for the other side.

Then, install your brackets in the bottom of your hand rails at the proper spots (where your blocks are). You can place your hand rail in place and mark the center for each bracket on the bottom of each of your hand rails before installing. Pre-drill your holes for your bracket screws, taking care not to drill out the other side of your hand rail. Then, using a hand screwdriver, install your brackets on your hand rails.

Now, while a helper on each end, holds each hand rail in place, predrill your holes and install each bracket into the center of your backing plates. Your handrails are in place.

Chapter 19: <u>Install Your Deck Boards</u>

Deck Boards

Now comes the fun part; installing your deck boards. This will give you a real feeling of accomplishment as you proceed.

Begin with the 1st board closest to the house. You will need to notch out each end to go around your posts. First, measure the width of your deck from the outside edge of each rim joist. Then, measure your 5/4" x 6" x 16' boards for length. If you are able, you will overhang your deck boards equally on either side of your deck. If not, flush is OK. Take the overall length of your board, minus your deck width and divide it in half. This is the amount of overhang on each end.

Place your 1st deck board on your saw horses and clamp down. Now, measure from the house to the outside end of your post on both sides and transfer this measurement to your 1st deck and make a mark on each end. Now, measure from the outside edge of your rim joist to the inside edge of your post, add in any overhang amount, and mark your deck board accordingly. Do both sides. Then, taking your small T-Square, pencil mark the notch that needs to be cut out on both sides.

Using your skill saw and Sawsall (or a jig saw), cut out your notches. Unclamp your board, set it in place, and predrill 2 holes in the center of each joist, 2" from the ends of your deck board. Make sure that the board is tight against your house. Then, install your board using 2 1/2" deck screws in each joist.

Put on your screw apron and load up the pockets with your screws. Repeat the process for installing all of your boards, cutting notches where needed and installing all of your boards even on one side (equal overhang on one edge). If necessary, once all of your deck boards have been installed, you may need to trim one edge of your boards if your lengths vary. Be sure that your boards are as tight as possible to the previous deck board installed before screwing them in. If they are warped slightly, you can screw in a 2" x 4" block into your joist about an 1/8" away from the edge the board that you are installing, and using your small curved pry bar, hold the board as close to the installed board as you can before screwing it in. Do this as often as needed. If you come across a board that is just too warped, set it off to the side for later returning.

When you reach your last 4 boards, before installing them, take a measurement of the area of your deck that is left to cover. Measure from the outside edge of the last deck board that you installed to the edge of your deck. Divide this measurement by 5.5". Any remainder will be the width of your final board. If the remainder is less than 1/2" or so, you will need to divide it by 4 and space your final boards out to this measurement. If it is more than the 1/2", then you will simply need to rip your final board along the length to the proper measurement.

Once all of your deck boards have been installed, take a moment to look over your handy work. I am sure that you have done a great job. Be proud of yourself and your helpers.

Chapter 20: <u>Install Lighting and Balusters</u>

Deck Lighting

Completed Deck

Deck Lighting

Installing lighting for your deck will add to its use by allowing you to enjoy it well into the evening. We installed our lighting ourselves, since I have some experience with electric. However, I would recommend that you hire an electrical contractor to do yours, unless you are absolutely sure of what you are doing. In those cases, no instruction from me would be necessary.

You can have your contractor add 1 or 2 outside lights on your house, on either side of your access door. Put the lights on a dimmer, so that you can control the brightness. You may want it dimmer for simple ambiance or may need it brighter if you are dining or playing cards or games. I would also recommend having a 2 outlet outside receptacle installed with a cover protecting the GFCI plugs. This will give you an outlet for adding low voltage lighting, as well as a second outlet to run an electric blower if you need to clean up leaves in your yard or an electric trimmer for cutting hedges and/or evergreens.

I would also install some solar lights on your post tops around the corners of your deck, along with the top and bottom posts of your stairs. You can use other accent caps on your other deck posts. In addition to that, you can install some low voltage lighting to accent your other posts, along with your stairs. This type of lighting would be mounted on your top rail under your top railing, just to the right or left of your posts.

The type of lighting that you will use is up to you. There are various options out there, so make your choices. If you will be installing some low voltage lighting, you should use your nail gun with 1/2" staples to staple your wires under your stairs, as well as, under your deck railing close to your rails. That way, it will barely be seen.

Install Your Balusters

Once your lighting has all been installed, it is time to cut and install your balusters around the deck and along your stairs. Take your 36" balusters, and cut the bottom end at a 45 degree angle leaving a 1/4" flat stub along the bottom for effect. Once they are all cut, take a small piece of 2" x 4" to use as a spacer, and beginning at the post closest to the house, begin by predrilling for your 2 1/2" screws, which will be installed at 2" from either end of your baluster boards. Install your balusters around your deck and along your stairs. Using your 2" x 4" spacer between each one as you screw in your screw, top and bottom, will keep all of them level, since your first one will be spaced off of your level post. Make sure that the baluster is tight against the spacer before screwing in, as well as, tight against the underside of your railing.

Now your deck is complete. Nice job. It should give you many years of enjoyment. You should now call for a final inspection.

Painting or Staining Your Deck

If you decide to paint or stain your deck, you should wait a full year for the treated lumber to dry out. Then, pressure wash the entire deck, let it thoroughly dry for a couple of days, and either prime and paint it or stain it with a quality stain that is guaranteed to last for several years.

Chapter 21: <u>Enjoy Your New Deck</u>

Your new deck should bring you many years of enjoyment. It is solidly built (if you followed my instructions) and be a place where you can enjoy yourself with family and friends.

If you are putting a grill on the deck, make sure that you set it up at least 6' from your house and 2' away from your deck railing and stairs. If you are putting patio furniture on your deck, be sure to buy something that is heavy enough to withstand exposure to wind. I would not use plastic chairs. You don't want to keep chasing your furniture all over your yard, or take a chance of anything smashing into your access door.

A couple of things that you can do to enhance your deck, if you so desire, is to put up an umbrella or gazebo over the deck to provide some shade during the peak sunny periods and some shelter in light rain. You can also use some of your leftover wood to build a box in order to store chair cushions. If you decide to do this, make sure that you cover the inside, including the lid with plastic to prevent water leakage. You could also build some planter boxes that can be hung just outside your top rail to add some flowers. Be sure to drill several 1/8" holes in the bottom of each for drainage.

Whatever you decide to do, the deck is yours. You built it, and you should be proud to enjoy it with your family and friends.

<u>Best of Luck in All That You Do!</u>

CJ Dodaro

Improving America LLC

About the Author

CJ Dodaro

I am a 68 year young man, who has worked very hard my whole life. Although I have occasionally worked for other companies, I have been an entrepreneur since I was a young boy.

I starting out selling things door to door when I was around 10 years old; seeds, greeting cards, and wrapping paper for all occasions. After a couple of years, I graduated to lemonade/Kool-Aid stands, washing cars and cutting neighbor's lawns. I did just about anything to make a few bucks.

When I turned 21 years old, I had the opportunity to purchase a portion of an existing landscape maintenance business from the gentleman I had been working for. I really enjoyed the work and soon built it into a full service maintenance and installation company which I operated successfully for over 25 years, before passing it on to my son.

I have also owned and operated a soup and sandwich restaurant, a gas station, and a body shop. I also had a three-piece 50s & 60s rock & roll band which was a lot of fun for many years.

Also, being a homeowner for over 30 years, with usually more time on my hands than money, I learned every aspect of home building and remodeling; from pouring a foundation to putting on a new roof and everything in between. I have installed tile, hardwood floors, carpeting, kitchen cabinets, toilets, vanities, etc. I have learned to do electrical work and plumbing as well.

Forced to retire at the age of 59 due to a severe back injury during a construction project, I found myself in unfamiliar territory; lots of time on my hands, but physically limited. So, after about 6 months of physical therapy, spending some time organizing things around the house, and doing some light projects, I began to go a little stir crazy. So, I decided to sit down and teach myself the computer.

I caught on fairly quickly and was soon operating a couple of e-commerce websites, selling **DVDs, CDs**, and miscellaneous household items. I did that for a couple of years and then began to learn about the **Affiliate Marketing Business**; another new adventure. I operated (2) different websites for that business for a couple of years, which I have since shut down, realizing that I could do more by **Paying-it-Forward**. So, I decided to teach myself how to **write and self-publish eBooks** so that I could share the knowledge that I had acquired from starting and running several of my own successful businesses and **Improving America LLC** was born.

Our website is: **ImprovingAmericaLLC.com**. You should definitely check it out.

Improving America LLC

Improving America LLC is a multi-faceted company whose main objective is to help entrepreneurs create and/or improve their businesses. We do this in the following ways:

- **We create step-by-step eBooks and Paperbacks about how to create and run a successful business, along with some books on specific types of businesses and projects.**

- **We are an Angel Investor in new business startups, helping deserving companies build their businesses into successful ones.**

- **We also invest in Tax Lien Certificates and Tax Deeds by purchasing these delinquent taxes in order to help Counties across the USA obtain some much needed funds for the services that they provide their residents, such as their: Fire Depts., Police Dept., libraries, schools, etc.**

- **We resell the properties acquired through unredeemed Tax Lien Certificates and Tax Deeds to rehabbers and house flippers, at a tremendous discount, in order to provide jobs, along with additional housing for interested home owners across the country.**

- **We help people recover Unclaimed Property that they have either forgotten about or didn't know existed.**

- **We assist people who have gone through a Tax Sale Foreclosure recover Overages that they are due from the sale.**

Those of you that are interested in becoming entrepreneurs, with a strong desire to be your own boss and own your own business, or you are already an entrepreneur who needs advice on improving your business, please click on the **My eBooks** tab in the main menu at the top, and explore the many helps that I provide.

If you own a budding company that is looking for funds to increase their business, please send me a **mini-business plan** showing me what you and your company are made of, along with the direction that you intend to take, and I will be happy to review it. If I think that it is a solid plan, I will gladly point you in the direction to obtain some funding for your project and I may even invest in you myself. The **mini-business plan** should be limited to <u>no more than 15 pages</u>, showing me the highlights of you and your business. Send your email to: <u>cj@improvingamericallc.com</u>.

It is my intention to continue writing more books, specifically geared toward starting and operating specific businesses and completing specific projects. You can be kept apprised of my current projects, by signing up for my **Email notifications** on my website: **<u>ImprovingAmericaLLC.com</u>** or you may personally **Email** me at: <u>cj@improvingamericallc.com</u> in order to ask specific questions.

<u>Best of Luck in Life and All You Do!</u>

Sincerely,

CJ Dodaro

<u>Other Books by This Author</u>

Thank you for reading my book. Please take a moment to leave me a Review at your favorite retailer.

CJ Dodaro - Author

You can click on each of the **individual book links** to be directed to view a **<u>20%</u> sample of the book**. My **Other Books** are:

<u>Being Successful in Your Own Business - A Step-by-Step Guide to Success</u>

<u>A (3) Book Series:</u>

<u>Book 1</u> of 3 in the **Series:** <u>Your Business Setup</u>

You will learn how to choose: your Business, your Business Name, and your Business Structure. You will also learn how to: set up a Home Office, set up your Bookkeeping, create a Business Plan, get your Business Licenses, choose and purchase your Domain Name, choose a Host, choose a Website Theme, and initially set your site up.

(See: **<u>https://amzn.to/39drLxs</u>**).

<u>Book 2</u> of 3 in the **Series:** <u>Work on Your Website</u>

You will learn how to create: a Logo, a Home Page, additional Pages, Menus, Sidebar Widgets, and a Blog Post. You will also learn about: Keywords, Images, Affiliate Links, Product Reviews, and how to best benefit from Google and Bing.

(See: **<u>https://amzn.to/2peamyc</u>**).

<u>Book 3</u> of 3 in the **Series:** <u>Get Social, Videos, and Money Management</u>

You will learn how to set up and work with: Facebook, Twitter, and Pinterest. You will also learn: how to create Videos, about Money Management, how to do your own Taxes, and how to create Additional Income Streams.

(See: **<u>https://amzn.to/39ixrgy</u>**).

Book 4 - <u>Write it - Publish it - FREE</u>!

Instructions for Writing, Formatting, Publishing, and Marketing an eBook and a Paperback.

(See: **https://amzn.to/2tk6mpl**).

Book 5 - <u>Make Money - Work at Home with an Unclaimed Money Recovery Business</u>

An <u>Unclaimed Money Recovery Business</u> **is the perfect business to run out of your home. If you are looking for a way to supplement your income, which can eventually turn into a full-time career, then this could be for you.**

(See: **https://amzn.to/2tvl2bi**)

Book 6 - <u>Make Money - Work at Home with a Tax Sale Overages Business</u>

A <u>Tax Sale Overages Business</u> **is the perfect business to run out of your home. If you are looking for a way to supplement your income, which can eventually turn into a full-time career, then this could be for you.**

(See: **https://amzn.to/38hq5ns**).

Book 7 - <u>Make Money - Work at Home with a Tax Lien Certificates & Tax Deeds Business</u>

A Tax Lien Certificates & Tax Deeds Business is the perfect business to run out of your home. If you are looking for a way to supplement your income, which can eventually turn into a full-time career, then this could be for you.

(See: **https://amzn.to/38lhmyl**)

There will more **eBooks** coming in the near future. You can be kept apprised of their creation, by visiting my website: **ImprovingAmericaLLC.com** or you may personally **Email** me at: **cjdodaro@att.net** in order to ask specific questions.

Also, you can see all of my **Published books** that are available on **Amazon** by viewing my **Author's page on Amazon KDP.com**.

(See: **https://www.amazon.com/CJ-Dodaro/e/B07NGTB1DC?ref=dbs_p_ebk_r00_abau_000000**).

Simply key in that **link** into your **Search Engine window** and click: **Enter**.

If you prefer to see a **sample of any of my books**, you can view my **Author's page on Smashwords.com**.

(See: **https://www.smashwords.com/profile/view/CJDodaro**). **Scroll** down to see all of my **Published books** and click on the one that you wish to view.

<u>Best of Luck in Your Business and in All That You Do!</u>

Sincerely,

CJ Dodaro

<u>Contact Me</u>

There are several ways to **<u>Contact Me</u> and/or <u>View or Purchase My Books</u>**. These ways are:

<u>Contact Me</u>

1. On my website: **<u>ImprovingAmericaLLC.com</u>**. Contact me directly at: **<u>cj@improvingamericallc.com</u>**.

2. You may personally Email me at: **<u>cjdodaro@att.net</u>** in order to ask any specific questions.

<u>View or Purchase My Books</u>

1. **<u>Smashwords.com</u>**

   - Click on my **Author's page on Smashwords.com**

   - **Scroll** down to see all of my **Published books** and click on the one that you wish to view. You can **download** a **FREE 20% Sample** to review each one **<u>before</u>** you make your purchase.

   (See: **<u>https://www.smashwords.com/profile/view/CJDodaro</u>**).

2. **<u>Amazon Kindle Direct</u>**

   - Click on my **<u>Author's page on Amazon KDP</u>**

   - You can purchase any of my books in the **eBook and/or Paperback version.**

   (See: **<u>https://www.amazon.com/CJDodaro/e/B07NGTB1DC?ref=dbs_p_ebk_r00_abau_000000</u>**).

3. **<u>My Website: ImprovingAmericaLLC.com</u>**.

   - Click on the: **'eBooks' tab** (on top). You will find a list of all of my **eBooks (and Paperback versions), along with a description for each one.**

   - You can purchase any of my books in the **eBook and/or Paperback version** through a secured payment method.

   - You can also leave me a **Review** for any of my books by clicking on the: **'eBooks' tab** (on top) and leaving the **Review** on the appropriate **Post**. I thank you in advance.

There will more **eBooks** coming in the near future. You can be kept apprised of their creation, by visiting my website: **ImprovingAmericaLLC.com**. Click on the: **'eBooks' tab** (on top) to view **Posted information**.

Thank you.

Sincerely,

CJ Dodaro - Author

9 798566 080369